Get All Tied Up:
Tying Knots

By Carla Mooney

NORWOODHOUSE PRESS

Norwood House Press
PO Box 316598
Chicago, Illinois 60631

For information regarding Norwood House Press, please visit our Web site at:

www.norwoodhousepress.com or call 866-565-2900.

© 2011 by Norwood House Press.

Picture Credits:
Maury Aaseng, 19–20, 26–35, 37–42; Jack Arrington, 21 (right); Karen Barefoot, 6; Markus Bärlocher/ Public Domain, 32 (left); Nathan Bauer, 21 (left); cc-by-sa3.0*/Guillaume Blanchard/Wikimedia, 8 (right); Shirley Booth, 17; John Byer, 5; Chris O/Public Domain, 14; Dangergirl, 25 (top); cc-by-sa3.0/DarthLarwa/Wikimedia, 30; Tamia Dowlatabadi, 43; Patrice Dufour, 13; Sir John Evans/Public Domain, 8 (left); cc-by-sa2.5/David J. Fred/Wikimedia, 24; Bart Groenhuizen, 18 (left); U.S. Navy photo by Mass Communication Specialist 3rd Class Matthew D. Jordan, 22; Søren Fuglede Jørgensen, 23; Paul Kempin, 25 (bottom); Christophe Libert, 4; Library of Congress, 12, 15; Jason M., 18 (right); cc-by-sa2.5/Malta/Wikimedia, 29 (right); Andrew Massyn/Public Domain, 7; Montanabw/Public Domain, cover; Carla Mooney, 44; cc-by-sa3.0/Parkis/Wikimedia, 27 (right), 27; Allen Pope, 25 (left); Public domain, 9, 10, 11, 23; Dani Simmonds, 36
*cc-by-sa= Creative Commons by Share Alike License

LIBRARY OF CONGRESS CATALOGING-IN-PUBLICATION DATA

Mooney, Carla, 1970-
  Get all tied up : tying knots / by Carla Mooney.
   p. cm. -- (Adventure guides)
  Includes bibliographical references and index.
  Summary: "A fun look at the knot's place in history, sailing, fishing and sports. Illustrations and instructions provided to learn how to tie ten different types of knots and what the knots can be used for. Glossary, additional resources and index"--Provided by publisher.
   ISBN-13: 978-1-59953-384-1 (library edition : alk. paper)
   ISBN-10: 1-59953-384-7 (library edition : alk. paper)
  1. Knots and splices--Juvenile literature. I. Title.
  VM533.M67 2010
  623.88'82--dc22

2010010403

Manufactured in the United States of America in North Mankato, Minnesota.
158N—072010

2678

Table of Contents

Rock climbers tie different types of knots to keep them securely fastened to their equipment.

Knots:
Tied to History

It is almost impossible to go through life without learning to tie a knot. Most people's first knot-tying experience is learning to tie shoelaces. From that beginning, most of us will learn to tie at least some basic knots. Others use knots as part of recreation or in their jobs. Mountain climbers hang from ropes tied with knots. Sailors secure boats and sails with knots. Some people even create decorative art by making jewelry and weaving using knots.

A knot is made by tying together pieces of rope, string or cord. The best knots are simple to tie and easy to untie,

Many knots are combined to make decorative items called macramé.

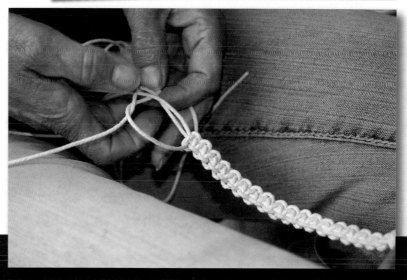

but they stay tied for the job. Different knots work better in different situations. A knot that is perfect for tying a package may not be a good choice to secure a climber's rope. In fact more than 4,000 types of knots have been tied throughout history.

Knots in Prehistoric Times

Knots have been around as long as humans have needed them. Researchers think the first knots may have been inspired by nature. Spider webs, bird nests, and even some plants may have served as knot-tying examples.

Early humans used knots to make weapons, catch food, and build shelters. For them, knot tying was not optional.

Spiders use many knots to make their webs.

Being able to tie a knot meant survival. If a hunter could not tie a line to a fishing rod or **lash** a spearhead to a shaft, he would not be able to feed his family. If he could not lash materials together to build a shelter, he could not protect his family from wind, rain, heat, and cold.

This South African bird the cape weaver uses knots to build a nest.

Knot Tying in the Animal World

People are not the only ones tying knots. Several animals are also knot tiers. Gorillas tie vines together to make their nests. Often they use granny knots, but have sometimes been seen tying a square knot. The weaverbird gets its name because of its elaborate nest. It uses materials such as leaf fibers, grass, and twigs to build a nest. A skilled weaverbird uses its feet and beak to tie dozens of different shaped knots and loops. Some animals even tie themselves in knots! The hagfish is a long, eel-like fish. When captured, these slimy creatures can tie their flexible bodies into an overhand knot that scrapes off slime and helps them escape.

Early humans used plant and animal materials to make ropes and cords. Strong plant fibers or vines could be used as ropes. Hunters also used animal parts for smaller ropes or cords. They cut animal hides into thin strips. Strong tendons worked well as ropes and cords. Because these plant and animal materials easily decayed, most early knots no longer exist.

This ancient Egyptian sculpture shows an elaborate knot in the belt of the male's skirt.

Ancient Societies

Over time, people created new knots as they needed them. They experimented with

A 19th-century Eskimo arrowhead flaker has a knotted cord to hold it together.

ropes and cords until they discovered a knot that worked for their purpose. The best knots survived for thousands of years. Knot tiers passed the methods down from generation to generation. Other knots spread around the world as people traveled on trade routes or entered other countries. Some of these knots are still tied today, such as the square and figure-eight knots. As knots evolved, the cord or rope, known as cordage, also became stronger. People discovered that weaving, twisting, or braiding plant fibers or vines made a longer and stronger rope.

In ancient Egypt, people used knots in many ways. When building pyramids, they used ropes and tied knots to haul massive stones through the desert and hoist them into place. Knots fastened the doors to the pharaohs' tombs. Egyptian sailors tied ship **riggings** with knots. The Egyptians were also accomplished rope makers.

They made ropes from natural materials such as **flax**, papyrus, and rawhide.

An ancient Egyptian painting shows a man sawing a board held in place by a knotted rope.

The Gordian Knot

According to Greek legend, the Gordian knot was a complex knot tied by a poor peasant named Gordius to secure his oxcart. When an **oracle** told the people that their future king would enter their country in a wagon, the people saw Gordius and his ox-cart and made him their king. Gordius dedicated his oxcart to the Greek god Zeus and tied it up. An oracle foretold that the person who untied the knot would rule all of Asia. Many people unsuccessfully tried to untie the knot. Finally, more than 100 years later, Alexander the Great arrived in the town. He approached the oxcart and the legendary Gordian knot. After first struggling with the knot, Alexander stepped back and asked if it mattered how he loosened the knot. Then he drew his sword and **severed** the knot in one stroke!

Alexander prepares to cut the Gordian knot.

Ancient Roman societies also tied complex knots. One of the earliest knots in recorded history is the popular Hercules knot. Roman doctors used the Hercules knot to tie bandages. One Roman citizen, Pliny the Elder, wrote that wounds bandaged with the Hercules knot healed faster. Today the Hercules knot is also known as a square or reef knot. Many first aid classes still teach the Hercules knot for bandages and slings.

In Peru, the Incas used sheet bend knots to tie fishing nets. They developed a system of tying knots to keep records of large sums and figures. This knot-record was called a quipu (KEE-poo). The Incas used their quipus to visually record numerical information such as

census figures, taxes, crops, and herds. Each quipu had vertical strands that hung from a horizontal cord. The Incas also used different colored cords to represent what they were counting. A green cord might show the number of cattle, while a white cord recorded sheep. To record data, the Incas tied knots in the vertical cords. Different types of knots represented different numbers.

North American Indians were also accomplished knot tiers and rope makers. In addition, the Indians used knots to calculate dates. If two people from

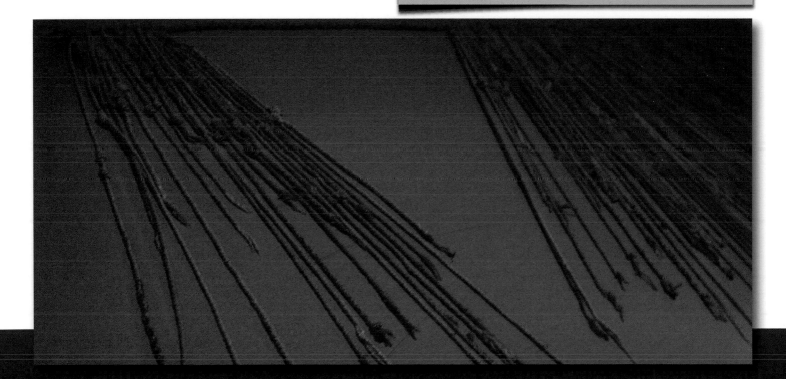

The information these quipus carried has been lost over time.

Sailors became experts at tying the many knots needed to operate the sails on a ship.

different tribes wanted to meet again in five days, they each tied five knots in two separate cords. Every day, each person would cut off or untie one knot. When all the knots were gone, the day of the meeting had arrived.

Knots Set Sail

Sailors have used knots for thousands of years. When dugout canoes became too large and heavy to lift out of the water, sailors needed knots to tie and secure their boats so they would not float away. With the introduction of sails and **masts** on boats, knots became even more important. Everyone on the sea needed a working

The rigging of a sailing ship reveals some of the many knots sailors use.

knowledge of knots. They tied knots to secure boats to their **moorings**. Knots and ropes attached sails to masts, formed **towlines**, and stopped sail sheets from flying out of their **cleats**. Massive 18th-century square-rigged

What's in a Name?

A knot's name often gives a clue as to what it meant to tiers. Some knot names refer to professions, such as archer, bell ringer, and weaver knots. These knots were probably important to people who worked in these trades. Sometimes the same knot can have many names. This is a hint that the knot may have been very important to different people and professions. Some names can refer to several different knots. When this happens, it probably means that the knots worked for the same purpose.

This stone relief depicts ancient Assyrian archers. A knot called "the archer" may have been named after the knots used in a bow.

sailing ships, whaling ships, China tea clippers, and even the British navy relied on knots to sail.

As boats and riggings became more sophisticated, sailors had to invent new strong and secure knots. Sailors on long sea voyages spent hours working with ropes and knots. Along with useful knots, they created beautiful and decorative knot and rope designs.

Today, many sailors use the same knots as sailors of the past. Other knots have changed as ropes have evolved. Some old knots do not work well on modern **synthetic** ropes because they are more slippery than older, natural fiber ropes. When this happened, sailors experimented and tied a new knot that did the job.

Knots Ashore

On shore, fishers tied knots in fishing lines and nets. Builders used ropes and knots to carry loads and lash together poles or other materials. A good knot helped a farmer hitch a team of horses to his plow or secure his prize cow to a fence. For these and other tasks, people used ropes and invented knots that were suited for the job.

Some of the most famous land ropers were the cowboys of the American West. To drive herds of animals, they relied on ropes and knots each day. The

A cowboy's lasso has a knot that will be loose when he throws it, yet tighten when it goes around the head or horns of a cow.

cowboys became sophisticated knot tiers, making knots and braids just as complicated as those done by sailors.

Knots Today

Today, knots are still evolving. People experiment and invent new knots every day. Climbers and fishers are some of today's most innovative knot tiers. A climber's life depends on his or her being able to tie strong, secure knots. His or her knots must also be able to be untied without damaging the ropes. For fishers, strong and secure knots protect expensive equipment or prize-winning fish.

Whether a knot is a new design or a tested old formula, the basic knot serves the same purpose—it connects. As they were in the past and will be in the future, knots stay tied to many lives.

Chapter 2

The Right Knot for the Job

Knots have different functions and are used for different jobs. Some knots can be used for a variety of different tasks. Others are limited to specific uses. Knowing how to pick the right knot for the job is the key to making your knot strong and secure.

• Hitch knots are used to secure a rope to an object such as a pole or post. People use hitch knots to tie boats to piers. They also tie hitch knots to secure a dog's leash to a railing.

• Bend knots join two ropes together to make a longer rope.

• Stopper knots can be tied at the end of a rope to prevent the rope from

Stopper knots are tied in lifeboat ropes.

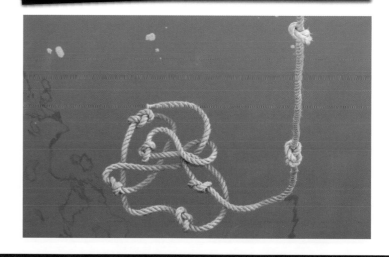

pulling free. These knots also add weight to a line or add grip to a rope. You may have seen stopper knots tied into a rope ladder. Each knot gives a place to grip your hands and feet.

• Binding knots are best used to fasten the ends of cords or ropes around an object.

• Loop knots join the rope to itself and make a circle. Loops can be fixed or slipped. This type of knot is useful for rescues or pulling a sled because the loop can be used as a handle.

• Decorative knots are tied for appearance rather than to perform a job, such as

A loop knot

Gifts are wrapped using decorative knots.

a bow on a present or in someone's hair.

Terms to Know: Knot Tying

Every knot is made of rope parts tied into one or more loops. This tying is done in a specific sequence or order. When learning how to tie a knot, you need to understand these words used in the directions.

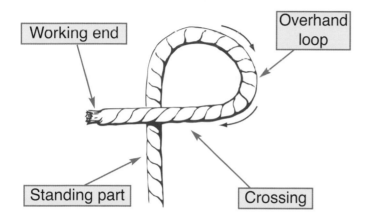

- Crossing – Any time ropes overlap each other.
- Working end – The end of the rope that you are working with.
- Standing part – The main part of the rope that you are not working with or tying. The standing end may be the end that is already tied to something, such as a boat.
- Loop – A crossing that forms a circle. If the ends are brought together, it is a closed loop. A loop with ends left apart is an open loop.
- Overhand loop – The rope's working end goes over the rope.

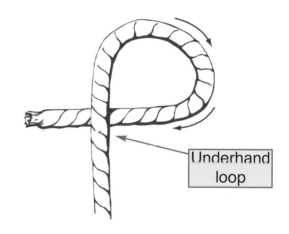

- Underhand loop – The rope's working end goes under the rope.

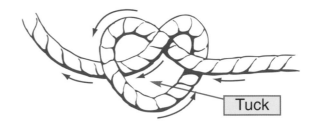

- Tuck – Push the working end of the rope into another part of the knot.
- Turn – Wrap the rope once around itself or another object. If the rope goes completely around the object to make a closed loop, it has made a round turn. Two round turns are

- Bight – A section of rope bent into a U-shape or a semicircle. It is a slack section in the middle part of the rope.

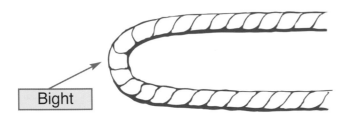

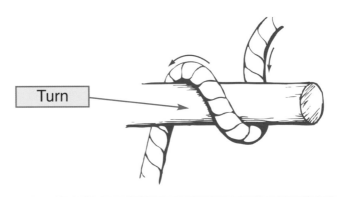

made when the rope forms two closed loops around an object.

- Eye – A loop made in a rope and secured by knotting.

Ropes and Lines

The type of rope, cord, or string you have can affect how a knot performs. Ropes come in all different sizes. Traditionally, rope is a line that has a 1 inch (2.5cm) or larger **circumference.** Cord has a smaller circumference. String or twine is the smallest.

In addition, ropes are made from different materials. In the past, rope, cord, and twine

Cotton is a natural fiber and a good choice for some rope and decorative bracelets.

A spool of twine

were made from natural fibers. People shredded and combed fibers of plant stems, stalks, and leaves. Cotton, jute, and hemp are all examples of natural fibers used for ropes. Natural fiber ropes did have disadvantages. They could be rough and thus hard on the hands. In addition, these ropes were

A sailor splices a rope made of **Kevlar**. Splicing forms a semi-permanent joint between two ropes. It is sometimes preferred over knots as a splice can retain up to 95 percent of its strength.

not very strong compared to modern synthetic ropes. The strength of a natural fiber rope came from its size. The larger the rope's circumference, the stronger it was. These ropes were also stronger when wet, but the water caused the natural fibers to rot faster.

Today, many natural fiber ropes have been replaced by modern synthetic rope. Synthetic ropes made from nylon,

Knot Theory

Knot theory is the mathematical study of knots. The knots used in these studies have no loose or dangling ends. Instead, the knot ends are joined to form a single twisted loop. One main area of study in knot theory is discovering the differences between knots and **classifying** them.

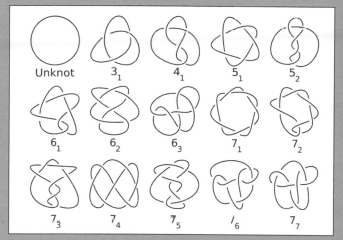

In this drawing, the string is crossed up to seven times.

polyester, and Kevlar are stronger than natural fiber ropes. They are water- and rot-resistant. Because it is so much stronger, synthetic rope can be used for more jobs than a natural fiber rope. Despite their strength, synthetic ropes are not perfect. They are smoother and more slippery than natural fiber ropes. This makes them harder to grip. Knots that have been used for centuries may not perform well with the new ropes.

Now that you have learned about knots, ropes, and how to read knot tying instructions, you are ready to start tying some knots of your own.

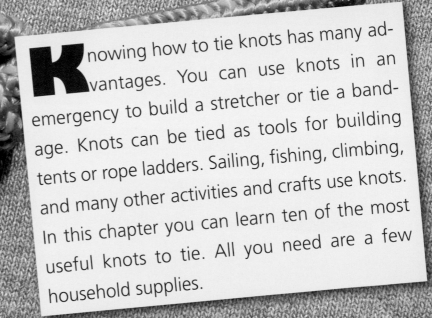

Chapter 3

Learning Knots:
Ten Knots to Tie

Knowing how to tie knots has many advantages. You can use knots in an emergency to build a stretcher or tie a bandage. Knots can be tied as tools for building tents or rope ladders. Sailing, fishing, climbing, and many other activities and crafts use knots. In this chapter you can learn ten of the most useful knots to tie. All you need are a few household supplies.

These are the materials you will need to tie ten knots:

✓ At least two lengths of rope that are about 3 feet (0.9m) long and at least ⅓ inch (0.8cm) in diameter.

✓ Heavy tape to secure rope ends to prevent fraying (optional)

✓ Sharp scissors or knife

✓ Pole or railing to practice attaching a rope. You could even use the leg of your kitchen table.

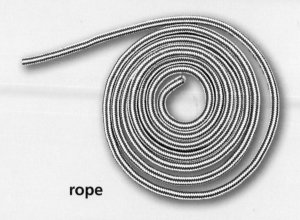

rope

heavy tape

scissors

These step-by-step instructions will teach you how to tie ten different knots. When tying a knot, keep in mind two important tips. First, make sure you follow the knot tying steps in the correct order. Second, before you tighten the knot, make sure to shape it so that it is in the correct position. Most knots need a little shaping before you tighten them.

Knot #1: Figure-Eight (stopper knot)

The figure-eight knot is a favorite because it is easy to tie and untie. It is also used to make grips on a climbing rope or to stop the end of a rope handle from pulling free.

Steps to Tie:

1. Make an overhand loop.

2. Pass the working end behind the standing part of the rope.

3. Pass the end through the first loop to make an "eight" shape.

4. Tighten the knot by pulling on both ends.

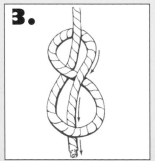

Knot #2: Overhand Knot (stopper knot)

The overhand knot is one of the smallest stopper knots. A stopper knot is a knot that prevents a knot from slipping through a hole. It can also prevent an object from sliding off a rope. It is a good knot to know because it is often used as a base for other, more complicated knots. It is good for knotting the end of a sewing thread or to stop a rope from unraveling.

Steps to Tie:

1. Make an overhand loop over the standing part of the rope.

2. Pass the working end under the standing part of the rope and through the loop.

3. Pull both ends of the rope to tighten the knot.

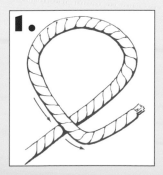

1.

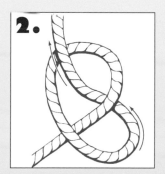

2.

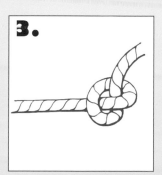

3.

Knot #3: Sheet Bend

A sheet bend is the perfect knot to join two ropes together. You might want to fix a broken shoelace or make a rope longer. Often the two ropes will be of different sizes.

Steps to Tie:

1. Form a bight in the first rope. If one rope is thicker than the other, use the thicker one for the bight. Pass the working end of the second rope through the bight.

2. Tuck the working end of the second rope behind the bight, then pass it up through the bight's loop. The working end of the second rope should pass over the first rope, but under itself.

3. Tighten the knot by pulling the standing part of both ropes.

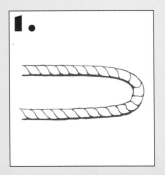

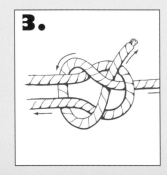

Knot #4: Bowline Bend

The bowline bend is used in all kinds of situations, such as camping, sailing, or climbing. It makes a temporary loop in a line.

Steps to Tie:

1. Make an overhand loop.

2. Wrap the working end up through the loop. Pass it behind the standing part, then back down through the loop.

3. Pull the standing part at the same time as you pull the loop and working end of the rope.

4. Leave the working end long and make sure there is a big enough loop remaining.

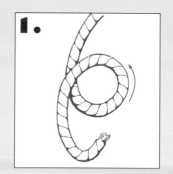

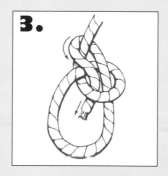

Double bowline

Knot #5: Figure-Eight Loop

The figure-eight loop is a common loop that can be tied and untied quickly and easily. It can even be tied in the middle of a rope when both ends are already tied to something else.

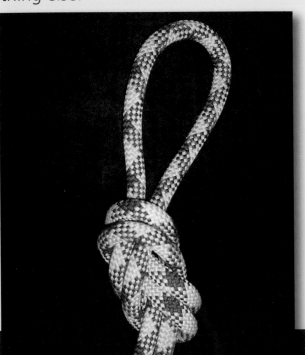

Steps to Tie:

1. Make a long bight.

2. Pass the bight behind the standing part of the rope and tie a figure-eight knot .

3. Adjust the loop to the size you want.

4. Pull on the ends to tighten.

1.

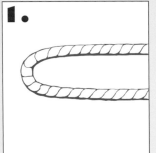

2.

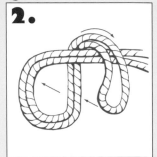

3.

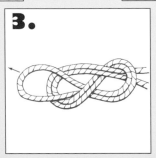

Knot #6: Two Half Hitches

This knot is simply two half hitch knots tied one after the other. It is a good knot to attach a rope to a post or railing.

Steps to Tie:

1. Pass the running end of the rope around the pole or railing. Pass the working end over, then under the standing part of the rope, tucking it through the loop you just made on the pole.

2. Make a second knot in the same manner. This time start by passing the running end around the standing part of the rope instead of the pole.

3. Push the two knots together and pull on the working end to tighten.

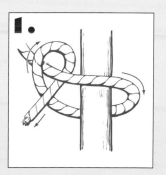

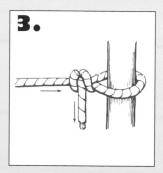

Knot #7: Clove Hitch

The clove hitch is easy to tie. It is not, however, the most secure knot and should not be used for safety or heavy loads. It is often used in combination with other knots and to start or finish many **lashings**.You might want to add the two half hitches knot to the clove hitch to make it more secure.

Steps to Tie:

1. Pass the running end around the pole. Cross it over the standing part, then pass the running end around the pole again.

2. Tuck the running end under the last crossing.

3. Pull the working end up to tighten the knot.

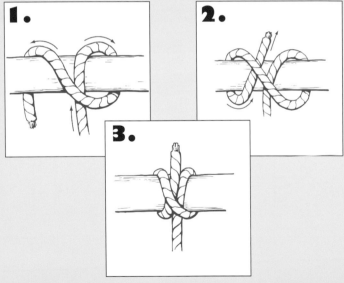

Knot #8: Timber Hitch

As you might guess from its name, the timber hitch is traditionally used when dragging logs or poles. It works best when tied around a rough, rounded surface such as a log. It is not a very secure knot, so do not use it alone if security is important.

Steps to Tie:

1. Start by tying a half hitch. Pass the working end of the rope around the log or pole.

2. Tuck it around the standing part.

3. Wrap the end of the rope around itself at least three times.

4. Pull the ends of the rope to tighten the knot.

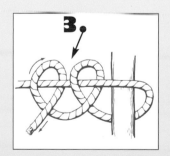

Warning About Square Knots

While the square knot is good for quick, ordinary tying, it is not a very secure knot. It comes undone or **capsizes** on itself when bumped, especially when tied in thick or slippery nylon ropes. To be safe, never use a square knot to join ropes that might move or carry an important load.

Want to know how to capsize a square knot? Just pull on one end in the opposite direction from which it came. Slide the end out and watch the whole knot fall apart.

Knot #9: Square Knot (binding knot)

The square knot, also called a reef knot, is often used to tie packages and bundles. It is also a good knot for tying bandages because it lies flat.

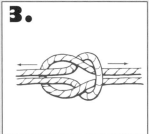

Steps to Tie:

1. Hold one of the ropes in each hand. Cross the right rope over and under the left rope.

2. Tuck the end of the right rope over and under the left end.

3. Pull the ends tight. If you have tied the knot correctly, both ends should come out the same side of the loop.

Knot #10: Constrictor Knot (binding knot)

The constrictor knot grips tightly when the ends are pulled in opposite directions. It squeezes tightly around a pole like a boa constrictor snake. It is good for tying small bundles or for tying a bag shut.

Steps to Tie:

1. Pass the running end over and around the pole. Cross over the standing part and pass behind the pole.

2. Bring the running end around the pole and up over the standing part.

3. Tuck the end under the center "X" part of the knot. Pull to tighten.

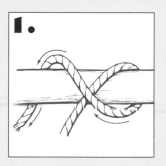
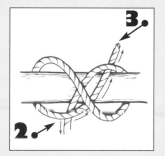

Now that you have learned how to tie ten knots, take some time to practice each one. Once you are comfortable with the knots, you will be ready to put your knot knowledge into action!

Knot Quiz

Take the following quiz to see whether you know the right knot for the job. What type of knot would you tie if:

1. You need to drag a heavy log across the yard.
2. You want to tie your dog's leash to a railing.
3. Your shoelace broke and you need to fix it.
4. You need to stop the end of a rope from fraying.
5. You want to make a climbing rope.
6. Your friends want to hang a tire swing.
7. Your brother hurt his arm and you need to tie a bandana together to make a sling.

Answers: 1. Timber hitch 2. Two half hitches 3. Sheet bend 4. Stopper knot 5. Figure-eight knot 6. Two half hitches 7. Square knot

Chapter 4

Putting It Together:
Building with Knots

Now that you know how to tie several different knots, you can put them to use. Lashings are special bindings that use knots. They tie packages and bundles. Lashings also tie wood, stakes, or poles together. Early humans used lashings to tie a rock and stick together and make an axe. You can use lashings to bundle a package, or to make a fishing rod, a rescue stretcher, a fort or tepee, or even tiny dollhouse stick furniture. To get started, let's learn about several different types of lashings.

Package Ties

Lashing is used in wrapping and securing bundles. Package ties can secure an object like a box or sleeping bag. They can also be used to secure several items such as a stack of books or newspapers. You can even use the rope or string as a handle to carry the object.

To make a package tie:

1. Tie a bowline loop at the end of a length of rope or string.

2. Pass the rope around the object and through the loop.

3. Wrap the rope around the object again, but this time wrap it at a right angle to the first wrap.

4. As you cross the rope underneath the object, use the running end to tie a crossing knot.

5. Bring the running end back to the front of the object. Pass it through the loop again. Secure the end with two half hitches.

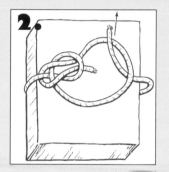

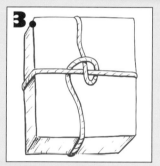

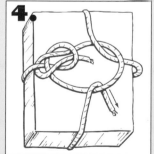

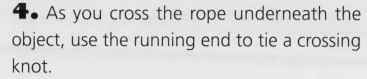

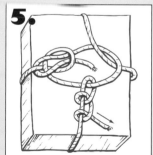

Round Lashing

Lashing poles together is very useful for making or repairing objects. Poles can be lashed parallel to each other or at right angles. A lashing should be neat and tight. Each turn must be drawn tight and kept close to the others so that they touch but do not overlap.

A round lashing binds two poles together to make a longer pole. This is useful for making a fishing rod, flagpole, or other longer pole.

To make a round lashing:

1. Lay your poles or sticks side by side. Tie a clove hitch around both poles.

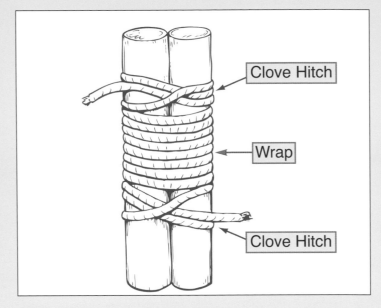

Clove Hitch

Wrap

Clove Hitch

2. Wrap the rope tightly about eight times around the two poles.

3. Then tie another clove hitch around the two poles.

4. To make your poles secure, repeat a second round lashing farther down the poles.

Sheer Lashing

A sheer lashing is used to make an A-frame. It is useful when building bridges, tent frames and other structures. This type of lashing uses a frapping turn. A frapping tightens rope wraps around a pole and holds them in place.

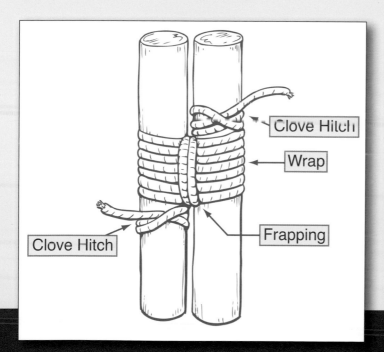

Clove Hitch

Clove Hitch

Wrap

Frapping

To make a sheer lashing:

1. Place your poles or sticks side by side. Tie a clove hitch around ONE pole.

2. Wrap the rope lightly around both poles. Leave enough space between the poles for the frapping turns. Make enough wraps until you have gone about twice as long as the width of one pole.

3. Make two frapping turns around the wraps between the poles. The frappings should draw the pole wraps together and make the lashing tight.

4. Tie a clove hitch to the second pole If the lashing is not too tight, the poles can be spread into an A-frame.

Tripod Lashing

A tripod lashing is a kind of a sheer lashing. It uses three poles instead of two to make a three-legged structure. It is easiest to tie this lashing on the ground and then raise your tripod.

To make a tripod lashing:

1. Place three poles side by side. Tie a clove hitch to the first pole.

2. Make several light wraps around all three poles.

3. Make two frapping turns between the first and second pole. Then make two frapping turns between the second and third poles.

4. To finish, tie a clove hitch on the second (or center) pole. Stand up the poles and test your new tripod!

Thief Knot

According to legend, many sailors tried to trick would-be thieves by tying their sea bags shut with a thief knot. The thief knot was very similar to the more common reef knot, and a quickly-moving thief usually did not notice the difference between the two knots. If a thief retied the sailor's bag with a reef knot, the sailor would know that someone had been going through his things!

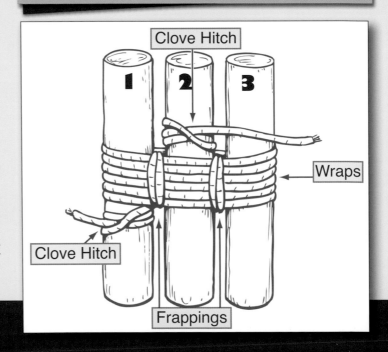

Square Lashing

Square lashing joins two poles at right angles. This type of lashing is good for making scaffolding, racks, or even a makeshift stretcher.

To make a square lashing:

1. Place two poles at 90-degree angles to each other. Tie a clove hitch on the vertical pole, right below where the poles cross.

2. Pull the rope up and in front of the horizontal pole. Pass it behind the vertical pole.

3. Pass it over the other side of the horizontal pole and then behind the lower part of the vertical pole next to the clove hitch made at the beginning. Repeat this over-under process four times, keeping each new

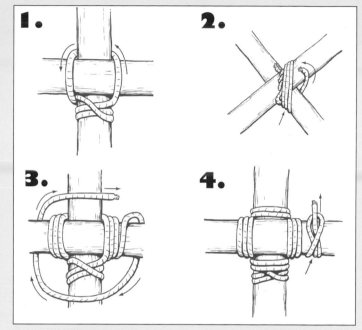

turn outside the previous turn on the horizontal pole and inside the previous turn on the vertical pole.

4. Make two or three tight frapping turns between both poles.

5. Pull tight and finish with a clove hitch on the horizontal pole.

Diagonal Lashing

A diagonal lashing is similar to a square lashing, but it is used when two poles need to be at an angle that is not 90 degrees.

To make a diagonal lashing:

1. Cross two poles diagonally. Make a timber hitch around both of them. Pull the timber hitch tight.

2. Next, make three vertical wraps around the center. The wraps should fall alongside, not on top of, the timber hitch. Then make three more wraps in the opposite diagonal direction.

3. Make two frapping turns between the poles. The frapping turn should pass below

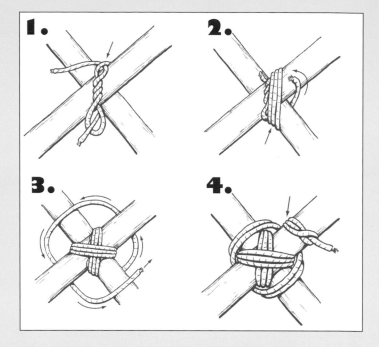

the upper pole and above the lower pole, just as they did in the sheer lashing.

4. Tie a clove hitch around one pole.

Knot Superstitions

Knots are part of many **superstitions** around the world. In some places, sailors believed that people with magical powers could tie the wind in a charmed knot. Superstitious seamen would buy a series of three charmed knots before a sea voyage. They believed that the first knot, when untied, would release a moderate wind. Untying the second knot released a half-**gale**. The final knot unleashed a hurricane when untied.

Some believed knots could cure disease. In some European countries, some believed that tying knots in the limbs of a willow tree could cure fever. In Germany, a person tried to get rid of warts by tying knots in a string. Then, the person would bury or hide the string under a stone. When the string rotted, the warts should have disappeared.

Try It Out

Now that you have mastered several knots and lashings, you can put your knowledge to work. Test your knowledge of knots and lashings by making model-sized projects with sticks and string. You can build a stretcher for an injured doll or a tepee or tent for action figures.

Doll Stretcher

Materials you will need: Four sticks, string, and a piece of felt or other material.

Instructions: Join the four sticks in a square or rectangle shape using a square lashing at each corner. After tying the lashings, add a piece of felt or material to the frame and your stretcher is complete!

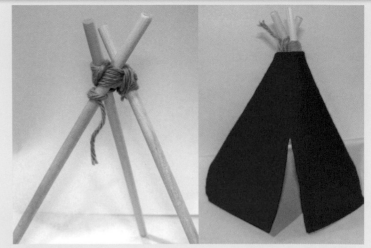

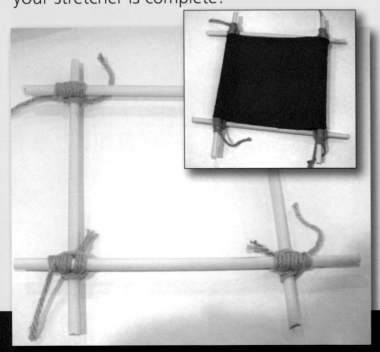

Tepee

Materials you will need: Three sticks, string, and a piece of felt or other material.

Instructions: Tie a tripod lashing around the three sticks. Once the frame is complete, drape a piece of felt or other material around the frame to finish the tepee.

Use your imagination to come up with more ideas to test your knot and lashing knowledge. The possibilities are endless when you start tying!

capsizes (KAP-sahyz-uhz): To collapse and fall apart.

census (SEN-suhss): A complete count of the people living in an area, state, or country.

circumference (sur-KUHM-fur-uhnss): The measure of the distance around a circle.

classifying (KLASS-uh-fye-ing): Putting things into groups according to their characteristics.

cleats (KLEETZ): An object made from wood or metal that has one or two projecting horns to which ropes may be secured.

flax (FLAKS): A fiber of the flax plant, a plant with blue flowers and long leaves.

gale (GALE): A very strong wind.

guilds (GILDZ): A group of people who do the same kind of work or have the same interests.

Kevlar (KEV-lar): A material introduced by DuPont in 1971. Kevlar can be made into strong, tough, stiff, high-melting fibers, that are five times stronger per weight than steel.

lash (LASH): To bind or fasten with rope or cord.

lashings (LASH-ingz): Bindings or fastenings made from rope.

masts (MASTZ): Tall vertical poles that rise from the deck of a ship to support the sails and riggings.

moorings (MOR-ingz): Places where boats are secured with ropes and cables.

oracle (AWR-uh-kuhl): A person who tells the future.

riggings (RIG-ingsz): The ropes and chains that support and work the masts and sails on a ship.

severed (SEV-erd): Separated from the whole by cutting or another similar way.

superstitions (soo-pur-STI-shuhnz): Things that people believe that are based on myth, magic, or legend.

synthetic (sin-THET-ik): Manufactured or artificial rather than found in nature.

towlines (TOH-lahynz): Lines used in towing a boat or other vehicle.

For More Information

Books

Penn, Randy. *The Everything Knots Book.* Avon, MA: Adams Media, 2004.

Stetson, Emily. *Knots to Know: Hitches, Loops, Bends & Bindings.* Charlotte, VT: Williamson, 2002.

Web Sites

Boat Safe Kids (http://boatsafe.com/kids/knots.htm). This Web site features step-by-step, animated instructions for learning how to tie several different knots.

The International Guild of Knot Tyers (www.igkt.net). The guild is an association of people with interests in knots and knotting techniques. The Web site has information for beginners, a knot gallery, and contact information for knotting events and guild chapters around the world.

Index

About the Author

Carla Mooney is the author of several books for young adults and children. She lives in Pittsburgh, Pennsylvania with her husband and three children.